PLATONIC FRIENDSHIP

: The study of attraction, keeping new friends and maintaining quality friendship

By

James Rascoe

Table of contents

I

Introduction

Connections are basic for the vast majority of various reasons, for example, expanding our profound prosperity, making solidness, figuring out how to be an old buddy or mate, having somebody to depend on and trust amid hardship, and somebody to vent to when we face difficulties, and companions and mates remove depression and make us. There is a wide range of kinds of connections. This part centers around four kinds of connections: Family connections, Friendships, Acquaintanceships, and Romantic connections.

Solid connections include genuineness, trust, regard, and open correspondence among accomplices and they require exertion to split the difference between the two individuals. There is no awkwardness of force. Accomplices regard each other's autonomy, can settle on their own choices unafraid of revenge or counter, and offer choices.

Close connections are those described by sensations of adoration and fascination for someone else. While heartfelt love can fluctuate, it frequently includes sensations of captivation, closeness, and responsibility. Specialists have thought of a wide range of ways of portraying how individuals experience and express love.

What Are the Three Most valuable Things in a friendship?

Closeness. You might consider the sexual part of a relationship when you hear the word closeness, however, this social structure block covers quite a lot more.

Responsibility.

Correspondence.

Chapter 1

Thinking back

How we have turned into the individual we are

How friends change our life

Companions are significant - they provide us with a sensation of having a place, bringing tomfoolery and giggling, loaning an additional hand, offering daily reassurance, and giving direction when you want it. Furthermore, regardless of whether you understand it, their impact works out positively past the occasion. Your dear fellowships help to shape the course of your life.

The following are a couple of ways that friends essentially influence your life:

1. Companions influence the manners in which you think and feel about yourself. Your companions' thought process about and answer you will, over the long haul, affect your view of yourself. That is, the point at which you're combined with an accomplice who sees you, as of now, as the sort of individual that you might want to turn into, the relationship

will impact you since it assists you with turning out to be more similar to your optimal self. You can likewise anticipate a comparable impact from dear companions. Nonetheless, companions who treat you less well will probably adversely affect who you become. Along these lines, remember this; pick your accomplice and companions shrewdly

2. Companions impact each other's very own inclinations and ways of life. At the point when companions share music and see each other's garments or finishing, their preferences can come off on one another. This impact may be moderately inconsequential, yet it could likewise have a more huge effect. For example, it can influence how you decide to spend your cash, like purchasing more things, continuing more excursions, or keeping it for later. It can likewise influence how you invest your energy, such as deciding to accomplish beneficent work as opposed to investing additional time relaxing with a glass of wine. Furthermore, companions can impact each other's ways of life, for example, their dietary patterns and how they focus on working out. These sorts of choices can straightforwardly influence your well-being and satisfaction.

3. Kinships in the current impact the idea of your companionships later on. I have seen many individuals in psychotherapy whose eagerness to be available to others was perpetually different by the double-crossing of a dear companion. Likewise, when individuals invest energy with companions who tattle a great deal, they justifiably will generally feel less trusting of others. Then again, I've likewise seen individuals who were careful about opening up to other people, and who battled with dejection, feel inspired and recharged by encountering a caring relationship. In this way, while finding and keeping strong companions is fundamental to being blissful, it is additionally critical to safeguarding yourself from the people who may, at last, let you feel be and are dangerous on the planet.

4. A solid informal organization is related to a better and longer life. Much examination has shown that individuals with companions and steady family are less focused on and are better off. A new report in the Proceedings of the National Academy of Sciences of the United States of America recertified areas of strength for associations that frequently increase individuals' life expectancy.

Given the various ways your companionships influence you, it's essential to be purposeful while picking companions. Does this individual have characteristics that you are searching for in a companion? How are they prone to impact you throughout the following one, five, or even decade? What's more, is that where you need to be then, at that point? Thus, when you are making arrangements to get along with companions, consider whether those are the connections - and that is the future - you need to construct.

What our previous connections mean for our present

11 signs your former connections are influencing your ongoing one

You might find you in some cases choose not to move on.

This could be because you're not over your ex-accomplice.

Or on the other hand, it may very well be because you're attempting to recuperate injuries from long ago by attempting to fix the past.

The following are 11 signs you are battling to continue.

The previous affects our present each day, whether it's by the way we approach specific circumstances, or how we genuinely respond to what individuals say.

In close connections, individuals can at times rehash ways of behaving to compensate for the falls of their past ones. In brain science, this is called reiteration impulse, and it implies you're attempting to fix the past by chasing after comparative circumstances or individuals who once hurt you.

There are a few signs that you haven't relinquished the past, and these can appear by the way you act with your ongoing accomplice. Frequently, these examples can begin amazingly right on time with the connections you had with your folks growing up. "Our life as a youngster encounters with our folks and our educators and our companions truly immensely affect how we work both by and by and expertly in early adulthood. "There's a quite huge populace of individuals who enter early adulthood who have frailty around making and overseeing connections. So I think what happens is the point at which you're not completely mindful of the examples you encountered at a more youthful age, you reenact those as a grown-up and once in a while it doesn't pretty search in your own or your expert life

We addressed a few relationship specialists to figure out how to let know if you're clinging to your past, and how this influences your ongoing relationship.

Here are the 11 signs :

1. You generally draw in similar kinds of individuals

If one of your folks was an egotist or a heavy drinker, you might find you continue to be drawn to these sorts of individuals until you can deal with what hurt you in that underlying relationship and start to mend.

2. You have spoiled delights

a terrible relationship can give you "polluted joys." These are things or encounters that were once essential to you, or that you used to appreciate, but since they are associated with your past accomplice you can't stand them any longer.

"Or on the other hand you feel regretful for getting a charge out of it, or returning to the same thing re-damages you, "Re-injury can be something typical, however having it endure for quite a while isn't ordinary. There's a major differentiation. There's generally this time of recuperating where you get this plunge and after that, you get an ascent. However, assuming you feel like you're continuously going to be in this plunge everlastingly, then that is not beneficial."

Polluted joys can be something as straightforward as a performer or a spot. It might be a thing of apparel "I can't wear this dress, not because he got it for me, but since he offered something pleasant about it or I wore it to something, "So in some cases, there's this culpability that you're double-crossing your ex-accomplice, and some of the time you simply feel like it's been polluted."

3. You have hang-ups around actual closeness

Once in a while, the signs probably won't be clear until you're in the room. Individuals can have sexual obstacles around their past connections in light of multiple factors.

"For example, when a person feels they can't be physically comfortable given their ex-accomplice. "We're talking about sex generally, yet in addition certain positions, or certain manners by which an individual contact them, or how they see themselves erotically Really critically, a major sign is if you tell yourself 'I won't consider it.' But assuming that it possesses you inwardly, around midnight, or on the other hand on the off chance that you're set off or pushed, it influences you."

4. You battle to impart about things that resent you

a propensity that can frame because of a terrible relationship is a failure to convey.

"If you felt that you weren't paid attention to in a past relationship, your approach to conveying may be more forceful than needed in the enhanced one, adding that this can prompt hatred developing.

On the off chance that you don't express right off the bat that something irritates you, it's just when it gets to a column that complaints are voiced.

"Did I say that that annoys me? Or on the other hand, did I pause, trusting it would disappear, until it got so terrible it caused a line between us?" "Hatred is much of the time a likely flashpoint. The absence of correspondence about plans is likewise frequently an issue... I think correspondence is a central point of contention."

5. Your injuries are not mended

Assuming that individuals copy the terrible correspondence they had in past connections, this can undoubtedly prompt savage columns. Individuals have close-to-home buttons, and this could be anything that disturbs their words, a manner of speaking, or disgracing and these are where your injuries are.

"Assuming that the injuries aren't there, somebody can express something to you that is disturbing you, yet it will not get to you to the degree it does when it's not healed," So it's vital to take a break at what your close to home issues are. Do you feel disgraced? Do you feel reprimanded? Do you feel not seen? What's more, anything that they are, just tenderly and empathetically take a gander at them and start to mend them.

"It's great to enroll your mate simultaneously assuming they are available to that, so say this is how I'm doing my life and I simply need to have the option to cherish you significantly more. I maintain that we should be nearer. It's truly brilliant when you have two individuals who are ready for that."

6. You're continually restless

This nervousness exacerbates the situation for individuals in every relational relationship, and one of the principal explanations behind it very well may be because individuals didn't play great parts models as a kid

You will generally think about things all the more literally, and all the more imprudently respond, causing a great deal of contention in a wide range of connections, "The normal response to tension is evasion, thus except if you had great models of individuals who are sincerely secure, and open, and can convey, really an expert must be mastered, and I'm seeing it's taking individuals much longer to reach a point where they understand they need to discover that expertise."

7. You disregard yourself

Assuming you had a previous relationship that was troublesome, oppressive, or lopsided here and there, you might disregard yourself because of the things your ex-accomplice said.

"We let ourselves know things like 'you're so dumb,' 'how is it that you could rehash this,' and we chide ourselves all the time like this messed up record in our heads, "But assuming you consider cautiously and ponder whose voice is this, truth be told, you'll understand it's not your voice. You've recently taken it on. It may very well be your dad's, or your ex-accomplice... This voice makes you question and judges yourself, particularly in light of everything the person said to you before, and it influences your way of behaving.

It resembles the previous keeping you in a crate, And some portion of breaking out of that container is understanding your previous relationship has zero power over you any longer.

8. You re-live and yet again make the past in your mind

In the wake of being harmed, you might find things going through your mind again and again. Certain individuals experience this so clearly, it's like re-living the injury.

"Re-living implies that when you neglect then, at that point, it isn't currently, and you're not in your current circumstance. "You can smell it, believe it, and it turns out to be so striking."

Large numbers of her clients experience bad dreams as well, like their ex pursuing them with a knife. This is particularly normal after an oppressive relationship because the victimizer has exploded in their brain.

"In the real sense of mind, these things have an endless space to purify, so this individual can feel like a beast. "On the off chance that this individual appears to hold a ton of control over you, I ask you 'might you at any point shrivel this individual in your mind, in this perception?' If not, they hold control over you."

9. You're continuously investigating your shoulder

If you went through a horrible or oppressive relationship previously, you could accept that everybody will be on a mission to get you. This is like"looking out for the bad side of behind each person you encounter.

"With injury comes this failure to trust life. "There are great individuals and there will be terrible circumstances that draw out the most awful in individuals. However, at that point, you must emerge from the suspicion where you're continuously investigating your shoulder."

On the off chance that you're with your accomplice or your companions, and you're continuously paying special attention to that time where they will entangle you, it could turn into an unavoidable outcome, as such, by being excessively distrustful, you could destroy your connections before they start.

"It's tied in with figuring out how to believe your gut, "And we frequently attempt to trust our heads excessively, yet the thing is our heads can legitimize anything. So when you end up supporting a lot about an individual I call it mental Photoshop, that is the point at which you realize your head is getting a piece made up for a lost time in this insane hamster wheel."

10. There's no trust

Assuming you were undermined before, an absence of trust can advance into your new connections, which can prompt various contentions, and, surprisingly, a separation.

"An absence of trust can appear in a controlling and jumpy way of behaving, "For instance, requesting that your accomplice see their telephone, [or to] check their messages or virtual entertainment accounts is a controlling propensity that will ultimately prompt your accomplice to be cautious, as you are attacking their security."

The most compelling things that make a relationship last are correspondence and trust, and assuming you're looking at your accomplice's gadgets or getting some information about them in an over-the-top manner, is a terrible sign.

"A great many people who don't have trust in likewise don't have certainty so you need to take a look at your self-confidence. "Assuming you know you're great and advantageous it's simpler to believe that somebody will suspect as much as well.

11. You drive individuals away

Certain individuals drive away their loved ones, and they can some of the time do this due to a terrible relationship, or injury in their experience growing up. this can appear as anxiety toward responsibility, concerning numerous this is a reaction to the chance of being harmed once more. You may be terrified of being deserted.

"You could observe that you are subliminally pushing your new accomplice to leave you, or request consistent consolation from them, which can become depleting and debilitating for them.

Continually driving individuals away could likewise be a sign you have an avoidant connection style, which is the point at which you enter connections that will definitely fizzle, or push away any individual who is thinking correctly for you. Along these lines, you never let anyone hurt you, however, you don't find bliss by the same token.

Chapter 2

Looking forward

So what can be done?

(Improving as an individual in a relationship)

Take some time

Individuals at times wind up hopping from one relationship to another, without truly peering inside themselves to see where a portion of their more profound issues lies.

If you don't require some investment to reflect, you may be going straight into another relationship just because you miss the closeness and closeness of an accomplice yet the new individual probably won't be ideal for you by any means. Regardless of whether they are, you probably won't be in the right temper to make it work.

"The main thing to do is to take as much time as is needed to mend, "At whatever point a separation occurs, whether a terrible one or a genial one, it normally prompts a profound channel. You are separating from somebody you cherished and somebody you invested a great deal of energy with, so you should find an opportunity to correct and once again figure out how to act naturally, without the other individual in the situation. Carving out an opportunity to find out about yourself and ponder your relationship can do a ton to assist the following relationship with being a triumph."

Recollect not every person is similar

Since somebody has harmed you before, it doesn't imply that your new accomplice will do likewise, and it certainly doesn't imply that you ought to rebuff them for the errors made in your past relationship," Brud added.

It's likewise essential to speak with your new accomplice, be transparent, and make sense of why you could have specific hang-ups or sensitive areas.

"On the off chance that you realize that you have been silly in a given circumstance, make sense of why you acted that way. "You don't have to carefully describe the situation, yet essentially recognizing you were off-base and conveying a craving to improve, will assist your new relationship with thriving."

Make sure to remain positive

Connections are difficult to work, yet as the truism goes, nothing worth having comes simply.

it's essential to remain certain about connections since they are a test, however, they likewise show us so much and give us the solidarity to change as needs are.

"As far as I might be concerned, it's very gallant to adore. "Connections are about "That. How might you adore another person, how might you cherish yourself, how might you respect your awareness?

"[Relationships are] testing, however, that is our specialty. To cherish, to find out about our spots where we want to recuperate, to be provided for individuals, and appreciate life.

Practice making and keeping friends

Making Friends as an Adult Isn't Easy, so I Came up With 102 Expert-Backed Ways to Do It

Hardly any things in life are a higher priority than strong, dear friends."Many individuals will stroll all through your life, yet just obvious companions will leave impressions in your heart." Looking back at the companions that have traveled every which way in your life, you can presumably see the value in how genuine that is.

While it may very well be trying to meet new individuals you genuinely interface with as a grown-up, with life feeling generally "ordinary" nowadays, we as a whole are wanting social association now like never before, and a few of us are longing for previously unheard-of bonds. What's the significance here? We're presently in a superb climate to make new companions.

To gain proficiency with the absolute most effective ways to make enduring fellowships, we addressed a portion of the top specialists and psychological well-being specialists. Here are their top tips for how to make new companions.

Step-by-step instructions to make friends

1. Step up / take initiative

Assuming you find individuals around you, you don't have to trust that anybody will connect with you and venture out. All things considered, become a benevolent initiator regardless of whether you're a contemplative person. Begin a talk with an individual and offer something valuable to them. Moreover, let them share about themselves. There's a compelling reason you should be so private at the absolute first communication, however, trade a couple of words or stories that can loosen things up.

2. Join another club or association

Engage in an activity that is important to you, where you're probably going to meet others with comparable qualities and interests. You'll have something to associate over and a portion of these connections could turn out to be durable fellowships with time.

3. Show that you're amicable

"An individual that has companions should demonstrate that they are friendly, "I frequently assist my patients with understanding that you should be what you look for. What characteristics mean quite a bit to you in a companion? Ensure that you are embodying those."

 4. Try not to search for likenesses

If you don't impart a comparable vision and leisure activities to somebody, it doesn't mean you can't foster a kinship. "A genuine companion resembles a profound sea who sees every one of the imperfections of someone else, "Subsequently, don't pass judgment on somebody if he/she has a place with an alternate outlook. Not doing so will permit you to make new companions."

5. Be a decent audience

Assuming you notice your consideration meandering when somebody is talking, attempt to take it back to what they're talking about. On the off chance that you're listening great, others will feel regarded, comprehended, and heartily towards you.

6. Make kinships with companions of companions."

"This is great if the objective is to extend your circle, "Many likewise think of it as helpful and safe since they presumably share a ton of the qualities of your common companion."

7. Keep in contact

Whenever you have interfaced with an individual and traded contact numbers, remember to call or message them. Call them and request the following get-together. Or on the other hand, you can likewise impart via telephone. Opening up to somebody oftentimes is an incredible arrangement to foster areas of strength for a — until it doesn't irritate the other individual.

8. Say OK

This is a rule entertainers use while doing comedy and it applies to making new companions, as well! That saying OK can seem to be receptive to attempting new things, yet it can likewise seem to be simply being available to any place the discussion takes you.

9. Increment your fearlessness

At the point when you are certain about yourself and such as yourself, it makes it more straightforward so that others might consider those characteristics in you to be well. Enjoying yourself and being in a sound mental and close-to-home spot is a significant stage before securing new connections. The objective ought not to be to just make companionships but to keep up with them.

10. Grin

Grinning while at the same time keeping an eye-to-eye connection with somebody will make a beneficial outcome for the other individual. Chatting with a comforting grin and predictable eye-to-eye connection causes the other individual to feel good and inspired by the discussion.

11. Find a gathering that is meeting on the web

If you would rather not participate in face-to-face exercises yet because of COVID, find a gathering on the web. For instance, there are online book clubs and business organizing clubs, and that's just the beginning.

12. Try not to set your assumptions excessively high or expect a lot from one individual

"While making companionships, I frequently prompt having numerous companions for different reasons, "One of the significant reasons is to stay away from mutually dependent connections and those that might arise from injury holding. Be sensible with your assumptions."

13. Help out for somebody

Research has confirmed the positive result of helping out somebody. It helps in creating mutual feelings and great energies between the two individuals. Indeed, even a little demonstration of delicacy can contribute a ton — like giving assistance or direction to the individual close to you, whether at work, school, or any friendly spot of some kind or another.

14. Ask possible new companions out for "companion dates"

"It might feel off-kilter or make you restless, yet inquiring as to whether they might want to get an espresso or take a walk is an extraordinary method for getting closer to them, "You could follow it up from there and live it up — or you could find you don't interface much. The more companion dates you go on, the more probable you are to find individuals who are a solid match."

5. Show up

Ordinarily, valuable open doors for kinships are missed because individuals neglect to be present. For a model, assuming you are welcomed out with colleagues, a nurturing bunch, schoolmates, or a neighborhood gathering, simply go. It is in many cases expressed that a huge piece of progress is appearing; this can likewise turn out as expected in fellowships. To make companions, you need to set yourself in the situation to make fellowships.

16. Take a stab at "reflecting."

There's a mental technique called reflecting and it includes inconspicuously impersonating the other individual's way of behaving. This can be replicating their non-verbal communication, looks, signals, and so forth. This mimicry works with people loving someone else and accordingly being keener on turning into your companion.

17. Be steady

Be punctual whenever you are making arrangements with somebody. Don't message them twenty minutes prior and say you'll be twenty minutes late, or more awful, drop without a second to spare. Little things like being punctual deepens trust in any relationship.

18. Know about social contrasts

As people frequently move for vacation and family commitments, understanding the way of life of fellowships inside your community is significant. While possibly not appropriately perceived, social contrasts can obstruct companionships.

19. Praise others

"Unconstrained characteristic transaction" happens when individuals will more often than not partner the descriptive words you use to portray others with your character, So, assuming you depict another person with positive modifiers, individuals will connect you with those characteristics.

20. Be interested

Pose unconditional inquiries. At the point when you're keen on others, they will frequently give back and fellowship can be conceived,

21. Attempt online entertainment or kinship applications

While certain individuals experience the ill effects of social nervousness and may battle with placing themselves in open gatherings at first, web-based entertainment is an extraordinary road. There are incredible gatherings that line up with different interests. Additionally, there are a couple of free applications that, very much like dating, interface companions — like Bumble BFF.

22. On the off chance that you're feeling great, show it.

Individuals are firmly impacted by the temperaments of others and might unwittingly feel the feelings of people around them. Give a valiant effort to impart good feelings so others feel blissful when they're around you.

23. Take input

Did your sister give you trouble growing okay with going on and on or for not listening well? Have friends and family let you know that occasionally you're a flaky piece? Focus on the signs individuals give you about how you're being received, and be available to find out about yourself. Your self-information will improve you a lot.

24. Be purposeful

On the off chance that you want fellowships, it's completely fine to be purposeful in your actions. Set objectives for yourself to make new companions.

25. Uncover your blemishes periodically

Individuals will quite often like you more after you commit an error, however, provided that they accept you are a capable individual. Showing that you're somewhat flawed makes you more interesting and shows a feeling of weakness toward individuals around you.

26. Be aware of how you're introducing yourself

This might appear glaringly evident, however, if you smell, are messy, or are simply messily introducing yourself, you might switch a few likely companions off. We as a whole have off days (it works out!) however introducing yourself with care shows that you esteem yourself.

27. Let them know confidential

Self-revelation is an extraordinary relationship-building procedure and assists the two players with feeling nearer to one another and bound to trust in each other later on. This weakness makes closeness in the fellowship.

28. Take a full breath before moving toward somebody or entering another space where you're wanting to meet new individuals.

29. It's typical for your nervousness to increase in that climate and making sure to take profound helpful breaths can diminish your tension and ideally make it more tomfoolery!

30. On the off chance that making associations with others is truly hard for you, think about bunch treatment

In bunch treatment, you will have a protected compartment to evaluate new relational abilities and get fair criticism about how others see you.

31. Accentuate your common qualities or normal interests

Individuals are more drawn to the people who are like them, whether in mentality, leisure activities they appreciate, or positions on questionable subjects. Find something you share for all intents and purposes.

32. Perceive that you don't promptly associate with every individual you meet, and not every person will interface with you

That is OK and simply implies that it wasn't intended to be, or a potential fellowship that could develop over the long haul.

33. Find a hobby (and we intend that in the gentlest way imaginable)

To meet individuals with whom you share something for all intents and purposes, get things done consistently that include others. Exercises can go from taking classes, joining side interest clubs, chipping in, playing a game or game, climbing, or any pursuit that meets consistently.

Individuals you meet will share your advantages, and you'll have something to discuss and partake in together. Try not to rely too much on social media. These can be useful to stay in contact, yet they don't supplant F2F kinship.

33. Get clarification on pressing issues

This is significant because it shows a real exertion in attempting to get to know somebody and makes you more agreeable.

34. Know about your non-verbal communication

It is easy to begin a conversation with another person if they appear to be more interested. Monitoring how we are standing (arms crossed, peering down, the body got some distance from others) can cause it to seem you are not open to meeting new individuals.

35. Try not to neglect individuals you know

While you're making new companions, remember individuals you know. Is there a most loved relative you might want to see more regularly? Call that person and recommend taking a walk, or to lunch. Are there colleagues working, at the chapel, in your area, engaged with your kids (or your own) school, or somewhere else with whom you could foster a fellowship? Consider connecting with them. Tell these individuals that you might want to share occasions and exercises.

36. Consider new ideas

Be available to frame new associations with neighbors, schoolmates, and collaborators, regardless of how unique about you they seem, by all accounts, to be. Having an assortment in your selection of companions keeps it fascinating.

37. Take the principal action

Taking the main action is alright. You can begin with a basic text like, "I am happy to the point that we got to meet today." If they answer, then, at that point, you have loosened things up. If they disregarded your turn, it wasn't intended to be.

38. Practice self-sympathy

Being caring to yourself will assist you with being kinder to other people and assist you in building companionships.

39. Eat dinners outside when you can

Rather than bringing your takeout back home or eating in your vehicle, have a go at eating outside at the takeout spot and grin at individuals. Welcome somebody to share your table.

40. In another companionship, attempt to recognize right off the bat whether it is corresponding.

Corresponding companionships offer the most grounded insurance against depression,

41. Act naturally

"If you are behaving like another person, who is the individual truly associating with?" Today you will be You, that is more genuine than valid. There is nobody alive who is Youer than You."

42. Converse with individuals in line at the supermarket.

Pose an inquiry about something they're purchasing, remark on what you like or could do without about the store, and discuss the wonderful blossoms in plain view. As well as assisting you with working on conversing with individuals, these individuals are likely from your area, and you could make another companion.

43. Visually engage with individuals while you're conversing with them

Individuals need to feel appreciated, and if you're not taking a gander at them, there is a higher probability that they will think you are not keen on their kinship.

44. Center around characteristics that you like about yourself or respect in others

Your character is profoundly molded by your companionship. Ponder what characteristics you like about yourself or wish you had, and search for individuals with those characteristics in your kinships.

45. Track down intriguing, fun individuals

Being associated with continuous action, and meeting with similar individuals consistently allows you an opportunity to get to know them before you choose to seek after a more private relationship. At the point when you find somebody you believe is especially wonderful, invest a little energy conversing with the person in question during or after your action. Pose inquiries about the venture you

are chipping away at, or sharing encounters and counsel. If you both partake in the discussion, and it works out positively, you can propose to meet previously or after the meeting for espresso. From that point, you can start to do more things together, until you've laid out an example of companionship.

46. Try not to take a sensation of depression as an indication of disappointment

Depression is the sign that you want to contact and reinforce your social associations, very much like yearning is the sign you want to eat. It's anything but a sign that you are doing anything wrong.

47. Be interested

Individuals appreciate discussing themselves. Ask them inquiries about themselves and see where the discussion leads.

48. Meet individuals at a bistro

Inquire as to whether you can go along with a sitting alone person, and except if they're dealing with their PC, start up a discussion about the espresso, the climate, or the climate.

49. Search for places that interface with your inclinations

Take a gander at the neighborhood tennis courts and check whether they have facilities or associations, find book clubs posted at the nearby bookshop or join a climbing bunch. At the point when you meet somebody here, you realize you share something.

50. Attempt another action

Is there something you've practically forever needed to do? Rollerblading, cooking, baking, carpentry, climbing, flying model planes, sewing? These exercises have vested parties, and they're likely to close by. Do an Internet look for vested parties in your ideal action, and jump in and let loose. You'll make companions quickly since you share something with all the others.

51. Be open

No one can tell where you will see your next "individual. So don't close entryways without seeing what's on the opposite side.

52. Interface on a local visit site, as nextdoor.com

At the point when you find somebody accomplishing something you like on the site, remark on it. Participate in neighborhood cleanup days. Heat treats, snap a photo, and say you'll be in the local park with the treats at a specific time and day. Welcome different neighbors to bring their espresso or beverages and go along with you.

53. Try not to avoid troublesome conversations

The struggle is an unavoidable piece of companionship and can prompt a more profound fellowship since you've dealt with something troublesome.

54. Show restraint toward yourself

All things considered, 140 hours were spent together to make an "old buddy. Show restraint toward yourself and try to invest the energy to foster enduring bonds.

55. Volunteer

Love books? Your nearby library could utilize your assistance. Turn into a docent at your number one historical center or display. On the off chance that you love kids, volunteer to take them climbing or show them something. Volunteer at your nearby nature community. There will be different grown-ups there you can be companions with.

56. Carve out the opportunity for isolation

Isolation improves your association with yourself and empowers association with others.

57. Pursue visits when you travel

Join a visit to any place you are or travel on a visit with different voyagers. You are almost certain to meet somebody who shares your movement interest.

58. Practice care

Care is an incredible asset to improving companionships. Fostering a care practice will assist you with building abilities to foster solid companionships.

59. Get the COVID-19 immunization

You'll expand your chances of meeting individuals assuming you are completely immunized. It will give you genuine serenity, and you'll feel improved going to new conditions.

60. Chuckle

Chuckling is quite possibly the best connector. Track down ways of chuckling with new individuals to make a strong bond.

62. Converse with individuals in the break room at work

Grin, gesture, say "greetings" and go there frequently. As individuals see you, they'll get to know you as an ordinary, and initiating discussions will be simpler.

63. Get the individual to recount a story

For instance, request them what the most fascinating part of their occupation is, what their number one spot in their city is, or what their #1 spot to visit as a youngster was,

"At the point when I meet new individuals, I view that as it's more straightforward to draw in them while they're looking at something they like or appreciate, and it allows them an opportunity to recount a fascinating story and offer pieces of their character such that it feels great to them. "Loosening things up in a simple or moderate way, and causing the other individual to feel great to share things in a discussion, is an effective method for beginning to move toward shaping a potential kinship.

64. Be truly legitimate

Genuineness fabricates endlessly, trust constructs closeness among individuals and this is an area of strength for a dear companionship. Academic partner of Psychiatry at the NY Presbyterian Hospital Weill-Cornell School of medication and host of the "What might I Do?" digital broadcast from iHeartRadio.

65. Practice sympathy

Sympathy is maybe the main social expertise and encourages association, and compatibility fabrication and is the underpinning of fellowship. Compassion includes imagining another person's perspective and pondering how they could feel in a given circumstance. It assists them with feeling appreciated, comprehended, and associated with us. Merciful compassion isn't just figuring out an individual's encounter and feeling with them but being moved to help if necessary and invited. This is the degree of compassion that can truly cultivate further kinships.

66. Be direct that you might want to be companions

Messing around makes for either a screwed-up or no companionship. Simply say, "Hello I like you, I might want to be your companion!" If this frightens somebody away, they aren't probably going to wind up an extraordinary companion in any case.

67. Reflect others' assets

Reflecting is a device utilized in treatment where the specialist mirrors back the positive qualities and characteristics of the client so the client can start to coordinate those positive perspectives into how they might interpret themselves. However long you are being genuine, reflecting a planned companion's assets to them can be a successful approach to building positive compatibility. The more unambiguous the perception, the more significant it will be for the beneficiary.

68. Have sensible assumptions

No companion can be ideally suited for you, address every one of your issues, or never dishearten. A genuine companionship has temporary obstacles with split the difference, conciliatory sentiments, and pardoning on the two sides. Assuming you over-expect, no fellowship will endure.

68. Ask for follow-up inquiries

On the off chance that someone is educating you regarding a new occasion, similar to a wedding or getting another little dog, request to see photographs which the vast majority have right with them on their telephone. This shows a more profound degree of interest and because words usually can't do a picture justice, you will have much more data to answer to work with a more grounded association.

69. Be available to new fellowships out of the oddest situations

No one can tell where you could meet somebody who could end up becoming a companion. An irregular gathering on an excursion, establishing at a similar game, talking at a care group, in numerous ways a companionship can bloom out of practically any opportunity meeting if either of you is available to the thought and take the risk to welcome the other to get together.

70. Search for what you can give, not what you can get

As you pay attention to an imminent companion, consider who or what you could realize that could be useful to them in some part of their life. For instance, assuming they say they later lost their employment, interface them with the selection representative, site, or professional guide who helped them when you were jobless. Consider what companions, associations, references, or administrations may be a help or asset to them and offer liberally.

71. Meet face to face

Facebook companions are not companions. Online corporations can enhance your in-person companionship … yet to develop the genuine obligations of fellowship you truly do require face-to-face gatherings and encounters together.

72. Concur with what others need to say and add to it

Take a tip from comedy and say, "OK, and...". One of the standards of improvisational parody is to answer others by concurring with what they have said and adding to it. This is because platitude, "no, however" will in general be a discussion plug and can bring the discussion down in a more opposing way. You shouldn't concur with something that is against your fundamental beliefs. What I am proposing is on the off chance that someone says it is cold outside, rather than saying, "All things considered it's not so cold as the week before" (which can feel like a shut down) take a stab at saying, "OK, it is freezing and I'm stressed over the blossoms I established last week." This leaves the discussion open for more conversation.

73. Esteem long-term kinships

It's perfect to make new companionships, yet there is something uniquely significant about long-lasting fellowships, you have shared a lump of your coexistences and in this way have specific references and shared encounters that can mean to such an extent. So reviving a more established, lost kinship can be an important

new and old companionship... find them and connect and revive.

74. Accomplice up with an outgoing companion

Go to occasions with an outgoing companion so they can assist you with making associations. Assuming that you are more modest or withdrawn, request one of your more outgoing companions to be your partner and assist you with meeting others.

75. Plan a new thing with another companion to foster the fellowship

New encounters develop recollections and closeness. Taking a stab at something, heading off to some place, or having an encounter that is different to you both invigorates the arrival of the neurochemical dopamine, the synapse of remuneration, which causes you to feel quite a bit better and needs more. This will invigorate your security and store memories that you can think back about later.

76. Attempt an irregular thoughtful gesture

See someone who appears as though they could utilize some cheer? Practice your mindfulness and effectively light up your day. This can go far in causing someone to feel unique and foster affection and an appreciation for you.

77. Put forth a genuine attemp.

It's a fantasy that extraordinary companionships ought to be sans upkeep. ALL connections, including fellowships, require exertion, time contributed, readiness to now and again do what you don't want to do, and talking when you don't want to talk. The work you put in will be the satisfaction you receive in return.

78. Sow the seed for some subsequent collaboration

Propose trading data and associating from now on. This can feel defenseless and be uneasiness inciting, however, it's worth impermanent distress or even a dismissal to ideally discover a few connections that offer enduring help.

79. Be excited

On the off chance that you stroll into a room and truly light up the spot with your energy, individuals will be drawn to you. On the other side of that, assuming you stroll into a room and put on a show of being dull and exhausting, nobody will need to interface with you. Individuals are normally drawn to others who emanate warmth, energy, and fervor.

80. Focus on being social something like one night seven days

Sounds basic, however, the more you're all over town, the higher the opportunity you'll meet individuals and make associations. Consider utilizing locales, for example, meetup.com to track down occasions in your space.

81. Mention an objective fact about somebody

The most effective way to initiate a discussion and possibly fabricate a companionship with somebody is to mention an observable fact and ask about it. For instance: "I saw you are wearing, that is an uncommon ascent. Where are you from?" and "those are delightful hoops." Do they have any unique importance? Individuals love to discuss themselves and all the more significantly, are complimented when somebody sees something about them.

82. Focus on a week-by-week club, class, or meeting or some likeness thereof

This can be random data or game evenings, book clubs, or intramural games. Challenge yourself to visit somewhere around a couple of new individuals every week.

83. Try

At the point when the vast majority stroll into a room of outsiders, they typically search for a calm space off in a corner and continue ahead. In the future, deliberately sit close to somebody who looks fascinating, and who you might want to get to know better and begin a discussion with them. The vast majority are hesitant to venture out. Assuming you loosen things up, no one can tell who you could meet and become companions with.

84. Offer a positive remark

Individuals appreciate being around somebody positive. Check whether you can remark on something you like or are appreciating right now.

85. Pose individuals more profound inquiries about their lives

This additionally implies being available to share a greater amount of yourself. Moving past shallow change will assist with developing associations.

86. Check out at individuals while they're talking

Especially in enormous gatherings, it tends to be simple for individuals to get ignored or not feel significant. If you are there offering consideration and showing appreciation with a great eye-to-eye connection, it will truly separate you from other people who might be on their telephone or unengaged in another manner.

87. Become what you wish to find

Be the companion you need. These are profound patterns of good following good that generally work.

88. Recollect subtleties

Recognizing significant insights regarding somebody (e.g.., birthday, canine's name) shows your consideration and capacity to 'do exist' with somebody.

89. Ask a colleague or neighbor for help

Individuals like to be useful and even though they might feel helpless, it's an extraordinary segue into companionship.

90. Be intrigued and enthusiastic about finding out about what they love

Pose them a lot of inquiries about the task/work/side interest they are engaged with. Ask them for what good reason they believe they should do the undertaking/position. Figure out their life mission and energy and be curious — seriously.

91. Utilize their name when you converse with them

This shows you're truly zeroing in on somebody and will assist them with feeling vital to you.

92. Contemplate the other individual's requirements and needs and accomplish something smart about it

For instance, to be companions with a specific music group, get passes to a show and welcome them to go along with you. Be a specialist and consider cautiously what the individual needs/needs. You will blow them away with care.

93. Lay out and implement fitting limits

It is normal to be an "accommodating person," as it's a human instinct to want that other to like you. On the off chance that you keep fitting limits, you'll just permit those into your circle who will regard you.

94. Partake in the occasion

At times there's a great deal of strain to have a kinship transform into a deep-rooted responsibility. To free yourself from that tension, you can simply zero in on the second and check whether this could be a companion for the present moment!

95. Look for weakness and association

Weakness is startling, yet people are truly made for the association. Indeed, even the most thoughtful individuals need closeness with others! The advantages outweigh the dangers.

96. Try not to think about it literally

It's critical to remember that most grown-ups have different needs. Try not to think about it literally if you're not at the actual first spot on the list while a relationship is being constructed — be glad to be on the rundown!

97. Step outside your usual range of familiarity

It is simple, particularly in present situations, to confine and remain in your air pocket. Accordingly, many are familiar with being distant from everyone else, and it becomes awkward to look for association beyond the safe place.

98. Try not to rush it

Any relationship will get some margin to construct. Remember this as you look for connection(s).

99. Keep "the brilliant rule" as the main priority

While it could be challenging to comprehend the reason why somebody is discontinuously hard to manage, consider what they might have happening in the background that impacts their way of behaving. Once more, don't think about it literally.

100. Lift others up

As well as having sympathy for other people who might be battling, approval is constantly valued. At the point when it is suitable, make a special effort to perceive the greatness you find in others.

101. Interface with genuinity

Kinships are tied in with telling the truth and being real with each other. Just discussion about exercises or thoughts you like or accept.

Try not to fixate on what you look like, or what you say to adjust to what you think the other individual needs to see or hear. On the off chance that you extend regard, and warmth and are true, an association will frame you and somebody you are meeting. Genuinity draws in other people who need to associate really, and these individuals will be your valid, long-lasting companions.

102. Put down your telephone and banter with individuals in broad daylight

It's not difficult to take cover behind your telephone screen and lose all sense of direction in the digital world while you are in broad daylight. Rather than doing this, when you go to your nearby bistro, supermarket, or some other neighborhood business you go to frequently, say "hello" to the specialists or clients, and make little discussion,

Making proper acquaintances or having a little talk with individuals you see consistently or a couple of times each week is a method for meeting new individuals and interfacing with others. It could be terrifying to put yourself out there and flash up a discussion, yet the prize is more prominent than the gamble. No one can say with any certainty that you might meet somebody who could turn out to be a companion forever.

Conclusion

Old friends are great for your well being. Companions can assist you with celebrating great times and offer help during terrible times. Companions forestall disconnection and dejection and allow you an opportunity to offer required friendship, as well. Companions can likewise:
Help your bliss and diminish your pressure
Work on your fearlessness and self-esteem

Assist you with adapting to injuries, like separation, difficult sickness, employment misfortune or the demise of a friend or family member
Urge you to change or stay away from unfortunate way of life propensities, like unnecessary drinking or absence of activity